PLANET MONSTER

Written by

HEATHER MAISNER

Illustrated by

ALAN ROWE

WALKER BOOKS
AND SUBSIDIARIES
LONDON • BOSTON • SYDNEY

For
my Mum
A.R.

For Adam,
Lizzie and James
H.M.

Zone 1

I'm a yellow demon. Choose me!

You have arrived on Planet Monster, but Mad Mathematician is already there. He is working on a plot to destroy the universe, and has set up a lab in the Underground City.

Your task is to find your way through the planet zones, reach his lab deep down in the Underground City and stop Mad Mathematician from destroying the universe.

I'm a red demon. Choose me!

Each zone has a number and two demons – a red one and a yellow one. **Start at zone 2, choose one demon and solve his number puzzle.** The answer will tell you which zone to go to next.

Beware! Not all routes lead to the Underground City. If you are sent back to the beginning, do not give up. If you can't solve a puzzle, there are answers at the end.

How many volcanoes
are smoking?
Count them.

Turn to this zone.

You have come to a forest where Flippies live.

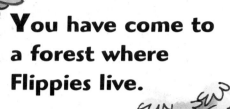

10 baby Flippies are climbing trees.
Can you see them?

2 spotted mummy Flippies are waiting below. Can you see them? Collect up the 10 babies and share them equally between the mummies. How many babies will each mummy have?

Turn to this zone.

Zone 4

You are on the beach with a family of Zimzums.

The biggest Zimzum has found 9 starfish. Can you see him? How many starfish has the smallest Zimzum found? Count them.

Turn to this zone.

Sea snails move in pairs.
Can you see 4 pairs?
How many sea snails
are there altogether?

Turn to this zone.

Turn to this zone.

Can you see the caterpillar sky-train? Find 3 Zimzums on the roof, 3 inside and 2 underneath. How many Zimzums are there altogether?

Turn to this zone.

You are swimming in the sea with lots of Zingies.

20 Zingies are swimming. Count them. 10 are wearing caps. The rest are wearing goggles. How many Zingies are wearing goggles?

Turn to this zone.

4 octopods are in the sea. Can you see them? 3 octopods are wearing 3 flippers each. 1 octopod is wearing 2 flippers. How many flippers are they wearing altogether?

Turn to this zone.

You have arrived in a town. Just look at those odd houses!

One of the triangular houses has 5 windows, one has 3 windows and two have 2 windows. How many windows do the triangular houses have altogether?

Turn to this zone.

How many houses are round? Count them. How many houses are triangular? Count them. How many round and triangular houses are there altogether?

Turn to this zone.

Zonki ghosts have 2 noses. There are 6 Zonki ghosts in the castle. Can you see them? How many noses do they have altogether?

Turn to this zone.

You are in a sweet shop with Zobbies

and Zimzums.

The Zimzum wearing orange has 20 Monster notes to spend. Can you see him? If he buys a chocolate bar for 7 Monster notes, how many notes will he have left?

Turn to this zone.

There are two Zobbies in the shop. Can you see them? If one Zobby buys a chocolate bar for 6 Monster notes and the other buys a toffee apple for 8 Monster notes, how much will they spend altogether?

Turn to this zone.

You have arrived at a city, but all the clocks have stopped.

You are in a restaurant with Dinozapps and Flippies.

Flippies are eating spiderbuns. Can you see them? They each started with 10 buns. Who has eaten the most buns? How many does he have left?

Turn to this zone.

Dinozapps are eating wormcakes. Can you see them? How many more wormcakes does the yellow Dinozapp have than the blue one next to him?

Turn to this zone.

You are in a cold, dark dungeon with a family of Buzzies.

There are 10 Buzzies here. Count them. If all the Buzzies with red spots fly away, how many will be left?

Turn to this zone.

Zone **14**

You are in a park in the rain with Plinkies and Dinozapps.

Well done!
You've arrived at
the Underground
City. But only just
in time.

Mad Mathematician has pulled the lever to destroy the universe and there are only 10 seconds left. But you can stop him by finding the correct button. It is above a yellow button, below a green button and between 2 orange buttons.

Answers

Are you stuck?

Here are the answers.

Zone 2
Yellow demon: 3
Red demon: 4

Zone 3
Yellow demon: 6
Red demon: 5

Zone 4
Yellow demon: 7
Red demon: 8

Zone 5
Yellow demon: 8
Red demon: 9

Zone 6
Yellow demon: 10
Red demon: 11

Zone 7
Yellow demon: 12
Red demon: 11

Zone 8
Yellow demon: 13
Red demon: 12

Zone 9
Yellow demon: 13
Red demon: 14

Zone 10
Yellow demon: 14
Red demon: 15

Zone 11
Yellow demon: 2
Red demon: 2

Zone 12
Yellow demon: 2
Red demon: 2

Zone 13
Yellow demon: 2
Red demon: 2

Zone 14
Yellow demon: 2
Red demon: 2

Zone 15

First published 1996 by Walker Books Ltd
87 Vauxhall Walk, London SE11 5HJ

Text © 1996 Heather Maisner
Illustrations © 1996 Alan Rowe

2 4 6 8 10 9 7 5 3 1

Printed in Singapore

This book has been typeset in ITC Highlander.

British Library Cataloguing in Publication Data
A catalogue record for this title is available
from the British Library.

ISBN 0-7445-3954-4 (hdbk)
ISBN 0-7445-4754-7 (pbk)